AF253401

Sound Never Dies and Other Poems

Sound Never Dies and Other Poems

C S Hughes

Il suono non muore mai.
Guglielmo Giovanni Maria Marconi

Contents

Birnam & Amber
Neither Read, Nor Yet Written
Train Station Number Nine
Here On Midsummer's River, We So Elegantly Fall
Harvest
Aberdeen Street
Looking For Yuri Gagarin
One For Sorrow

L C Smith & Corona Typewriters Inc

Vainglory Morning

In the atrium
the statues grow
life moving slow as sundials
faces blind
even when the painted eyes
of their subjects blink
the tears away and light
slanting from the transom window
the morning vainglory gold
but the marble
translucent as a sigh

Me & Willow One Evening

Willow laughs
in cicada afternoons
she swings her strangler's hair
to cage the falling sun
for a while, we both hang in the air
in disturbing equilibrium

She calls again to demand
of orb-mad eyes and awkward frown
that I tumble from the harbour of her limbs
that I go naked-handed
to fish the moon from out the pond

Though the scars of her eyes are par-blind
she scowls a twisty mouth
She does not see it dripping in my arms
how bright, how dark she sleeps

Coffee & Dinosaurs

The clock radio gently sounds
a fraught Carpenters song
echoing with the decaying glossolalia
left from the shores of dreaming
I dismiss, with a vagabond hand
the outré world a fraction longer
the morning light draws out my face
dismayed as abattoir horses

From below thin blankets
the sky is full of holes
a saw blade kind of sea
of embattled threads
safely, safely drowning

A seismic hand
writes slow rumbled words
I will look
upside down
until the sky becomes another land

Kettles no longer sing
a kindness, I suppose
but the coffee, so often now
stagnant as the immersive death
of mired dinosaurs
left too long, leaves a lukewarm coagulation
on a morning silent tongue

Morning's Blackbirds

In morning rain the road
keeps pieces of the night
not yet slicked with the marbling of passing cars
just a smattering
of lights on gravelled stones
a few stray stars
I suppose the gods forgot

I wash my face in the street
shouting at the chimney smoke and cold
with the mournful blackbirds watching on
they have only
half a wary song
waiting for the ripple
of my face to go
so they may in returning peace
(a doorway's brief respite)
dismay their own reflections

Yesterday, Today, Tomorrow

You have the look of ivoried lace
as if the wandered sun slow stained
where you pretend to hide
all the years marked in your face
the curtains in a discontent disclose
a pretence of a summer's day
the sun on jostling leaves
limned in expectation
a man stops at the gate
nondescript —thinks, moves away

Traffic rumbles in your throat
even sparrows start
as if a lion roared
the morning rain has a shy insouciance
until it heaves and impudently falls
obliterating the remnants
of a barely started glimpse
in the trammelled glass
of a promised morrow
and a bare remembered yesterday

Steel-Belted Radial

Imagine if roads remembered
every vibration cut by passing cars

A journey music
in palimpsest confusion
tyre treads worn thin
to the unravelling semblance
of sunsets in passing

Where just a thread remains
the ribs exposed beneath

As if some gathering devastation
bared at last the monster in the wheel

Holes big as eyes
in the harried side
of a withered world

The evening sun has filled me up
til I am red and full
livid mottle skin

Tongue slowly touching lips
a prehistoric heat
disgorged with a lizard compulsion

In the wreckage swollen night
whirring until still

On The Rebound

I will tell you the spheres of Newton's Cradle
are propelled by the weight of love
restrained and directed by desire's chains
suspended in a moment of unrequited apogee
in incalculable increments
falling again
deranged by conflict and too familiar contempt

You will say
on a restricted plane
it is the conservation of momentum by kinetic energy
that measures the velocities of two perfectly colliding
                                                      elastic
objects
from collision to equilibrium to this amplitude's maximum
in an imperfect calculation
heat, sound and friction dissipate

I will ask what hand
this initial impetus makes
you will whisper closely in my ear
from this bare math
we can barely intimate

Long Days Walking Down The Gulliver Road

The chimney red has leached
into the criss-cross mortar
as if the bricks were morning soft
and steepled with complaints

A bird high on the aerial
listening for god
flicks a wary eye
as if I came with shot and tar
to paint the sky

I have passed by
a million years
if you count distance in repeated aches
the chimneys lean like afternoons
a little farther

The same bird watching, silver-grey
perhaps
a different god
gone with stars about her neck
rising in the evening

Specola Vaticana (for George Coyne)

Perhaps with Galileo you would repair in shame
if time moved more slowly and less wise
than sidereal uncertainties
would you recant for a flawed design
a new suspect vehemence?

God is not a dictator, keeping martial time
but measured in the parallax
of our fixed and certain stars

We tear our fingernails
a razor to an ageless equanimity
this new and complex disorder
necessitates a carnivore

With few qualms, the heavens allow
though the waning shape
of an inalienable moon abides

In Rome We Gather Stones Like A Warning

An old librarian's hands are stained with words
quite invisible but ingrained
beneath the skin a microfiche translucence
where histories and prodigies entertain
like the ghosts of carnival
on the whorls of the Campo de Fiori

In Rome we heard them singing
the cobbles have lain a thousand years
in shapes lionesque and serpentine
as if berthed underneath
in homage and in death
still its shining skin
a lost chimera

We will draw truths from Virgil's disembodied pages
watch them in obeisance and in burning
until in the fragments that remain
with stern Bruno frowning from his shroud
we almost grasp this oracle
in our hands gone to ash
facile is the descent

Black-handed and forewarned
we gather sampietrino
hold them high as if
we are not the barricade but the road

From maligned stones, ringing
I can hear the blows
of the mallets that made them

Wielded with a stiletto and fragmentary love
as ravaged as the face of Michelangelo

In The Dusty Evening

Judy Wardrobe has in rows
her tattered days hung on hooks
with all her faded unbuttoned clothes

She tries them on and dances for a while
in the light of half-imagined days
the perfumes arranged on her trousseau
all smell like whales and funerals
with a sea deep note
of unrequited burial

You have strange translucent teeth
like fossils hardened into glass
I suspect some wickedness
has jewelled your smile so

How it must break when you bite
on life's dry and withered fruit
my darling though I can dance
in the dark and bright of stranger days
fading like the curtains til
from these ivory holes and threads
I am quite indistinguishable

Still, when I taste with savage laugh
the morsel lives that come here past
bringing sops and sympathy
my small sharp bites make small sharp work
of your face and hollow throat

In my ward I hang such spidered coats
that I may dance their days gone by
in this dusty evening

This Poem Is A War Crime

The prisoners have butterflies for mouths
teeth bared like burnt-out buildings
they say exactly what we want
– without undue coercion
just the slightest quaver
of the jaw and throat
where stubble hides the muzzled bruises
We lied, we are wrong
we came to drink your blood
these are eyes not camouflage
in haloes on our wings
Here the children have hands of bone
bandannas over nose and mouth
in the stench they forgot somehow to sing
The sun is bright in vain
inviolate on the mountainside
The studio has that flicker scent
Of blitzkrieg and cigars
when you are almost halfway up
back arched in trapezoid envy
the sky is less steady than it seems
Icarine- the too harsh blue
of interrupted broadcasts
Looking up, we make new stars
name them in bravado
see the smithereens
cascade in new intaglios
on the surface of the eye

blink the warmth of tears
gravity has an equivocal grip
when you are almost halfway down
knuckles raw as dinosaurs
feet arched in Quetzalcoatl torsions
sending hubris, sending love
we will solve this war
like a misheard refrain
that thick comforting savour
of something on the stove
notes played and played and played again
til, despite what we have heard
what we hear is right
what we hear now has
eternally been right

The War At Easter

The milk tastes off in wartime
clammy on the tongue
even when you are so distant
you can hardly hear the metal bend
You make *galaktoboureko*
so thick the shape returns
wondering why Easter
falls in archaic calendars
each year on new days
as if martyrdom were inexact in its demands
I imagine Medea's tears
in thick and sweet and distilled stains
when she learned she ate her young
Time Is a wolf, you say
and in one deft hand
break another egg

Fire & Glass

The morning is made of glass
rain cats softly pawing
I make my offering to the birds
they once again disdain my hand
return a wary, bright vibrato
of songs and heartbeat wings
for thrown seeds and stale bread

It is enough, the rain cats bite
at bare neck and upturned cheek
with sharp, dissolving bites
that sting with love and other warnings

The sparrows fall up and down, as if
inverting gravity, they fell
to Prometheus's lips

I am tied against the earth
the rain cats dance around me

Death of Leaves

In your chest I think I hear the sea
a far siren sounding
perhaps death is a shell
some strange worm inside
this silver nacre growing
from a season full of holes
toward hard winter

We harvest autumn colours
not for provender, nor feast
but to curtail a moment's thought
of a child lost and falling through the leaves

Here, a barrow full
with pale hands and warm embrace
as if from rot and skeleton and earth
the reckless knot of a long forgotten love
a strange smell like birth
of ungainly monsters

We gather our defence
neat lawns and ordered paths
in toy land plastic bins
in the shimmer smoke
of the furnace burning

Underpass

Graffiti plays a jagged game
as if fire
in its throes
were unrepentant

In a hole in a wall
I saw a church
softy glowing

Red with pilot lights and Judas fish
from pierced brass
scattered, chasing

Count a red flicker presence

If your hair falls out
it means someone wants you dead
the old sawtooth says

Fire turns to ash you comb through
looking for
a lost glint of colour

Finding, in your hands
a peaceful season

They gave the paroled prisoners
new suits and shoes
in charcoal drab and patent leather
and spoke them harshly

I will sleep
with the weight of mountains

A god semblanced, autonomic
in every changing traffic light

And a sky still open
with the flights of birds

Ghosts of Morning (An Enso)

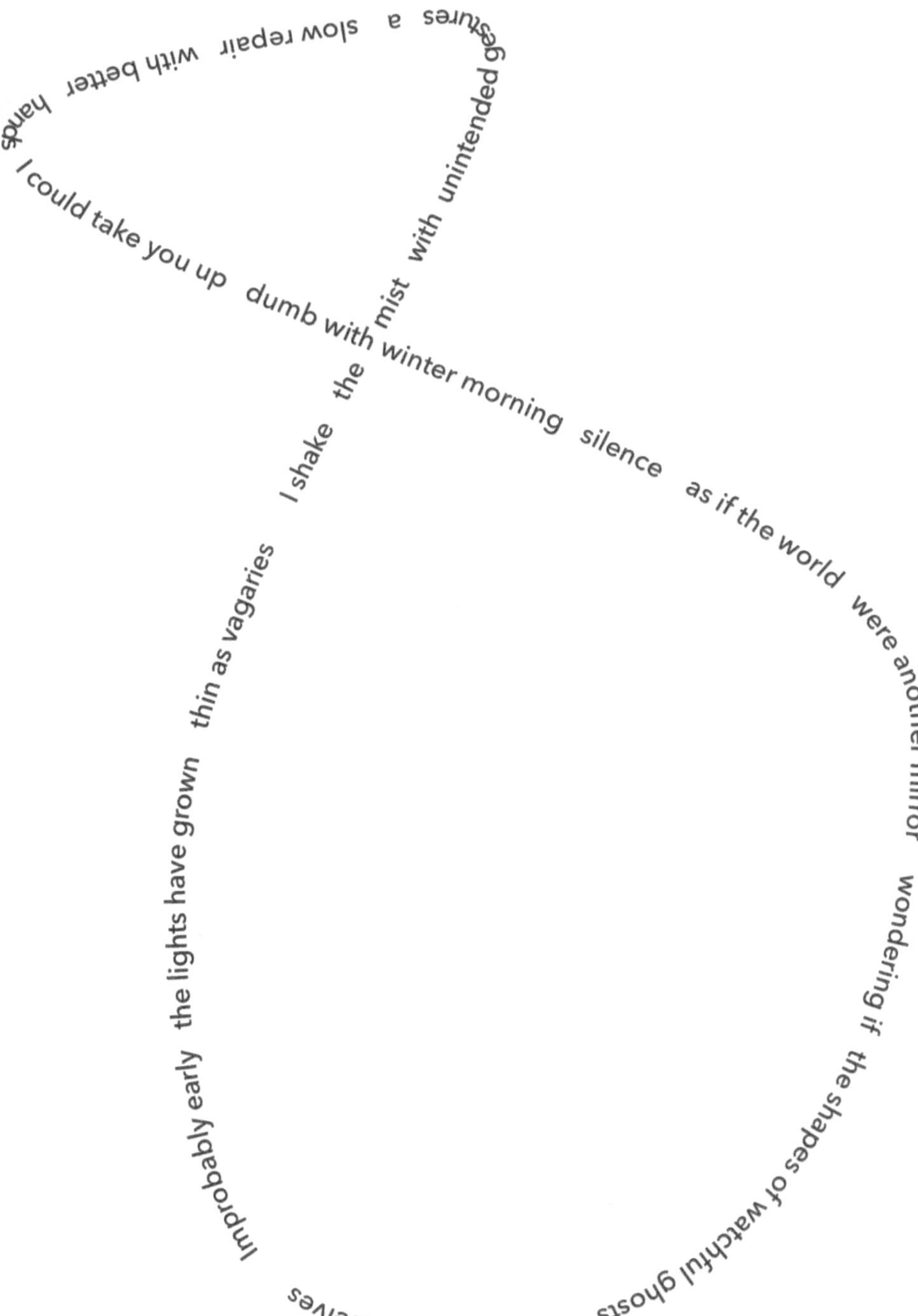

Toy Drum

A quiet child
bangs a drum
is beaten soundly
sent to hell
A noisy child
beats a drum
is given sugar
and a gun
A lonely child
drums a drum
breaks a smile
is left alone
An angry child
breaks a drum
is sent to Bedlam
now quite glum
A mooncalf child
hears a drum
dances while
her light has shone

Sound Never Dies

Il suono non muore mai
Marconi said, the reverberations
go on and on, only weakening when
deflected by the hard curvature
of the earth and the ionosphere
the surfaces between
blunt and cruel and with
the endured grain of weary blasphemies
attenuated and absorbed
confessions knotted in the wood
I can feel the echoing
burn it down
I hope one day to hear
the sermon on the mount
in a voice of fire
But, when finally we calibrated
a circuitry to listen
all we heard were the hammer blows
and amid the guttural shouts
of a language, almost lost
the sun raw throat of too familiar laughter

Petals

If you eat these petals, before retiring
through properties as yet unbeknownst to modern science
sight will be restored
Mrs A Clarke of Winnipeg, Manitoba saw meteors on
a new horizon, she thought the chariots had arrived
Short-sightedness completely cured
Mr Robertson of Saskatchewan
saw the grain of skin
like an isthmus in his child's hand
held firmly to cross highway 26, sick with salted ice
from the woods near François Xavier
home where the fire was the orange
of his mother's tongue, bright and black
with summer's laughing frozen fruit
spilled accidentally in the kitchen sink
dishes high as Babylon
the far-sought malaise, gone in the panchromatic
wilderness of criss-crossing lines
Sarah Clawson, aged fifty-four, of Mobile, Alabama
insomniac and half-prayered with macular degeneration
reversed the waterfall rush, the flowers broken
steeped, in a kind of tea, with sugar cubes
she could still get, because the factory was old fashioned
a bitter taste, but despite the door, quite crooked
swinging in the magnolia breeze
I guess, praise be, the frame's bent too, she writes
in her thank-you note, vision now restored
the distortions in her peripheries
where the dead once talked

almost completely smooth because
with a firm but gentle hand, the jags of fractures spreading
she crushed to sintered aromats
these falling petals

Fishbone Afternoon

We kill the afternoon
with the ritual and shape
of sparrows singing

As they bathe in sand
spilling from wings like water
imagining how cruel dolphins
no bigger than cupped hands

After we pick
the cathedral bones
quite bare of pale flesh
we wrapped the crucifix
in greasy headlines
the ink irrational and almost clear
the hollow eye still staring
as if another placid and airless life
disappointing gulls
were soon to begin

A mouth querulous in the face
of unctuous accusations

In the fragmentary evening sky
fishbone clouds
past sailing

Morsels Of A Candy-Coloured Day

Make a patter
Like the rain
In the shroud
Of battleship skies
Rust and proud
Traffic lights
Red as sweets
Said to stop
Stamp your yellow
Rubber-booted feet
You never once obeyed
Skipping puddles
To unmake
The bright-smeared day
Face big with lion's envy
Where hot breath
On marchpane windows
Makes a ghost evaporate
From the crowd
Of passing grey-skinned people
Cradling covet morsels
For some other rainless child

A Game With The Ghost Of Another Falling Evening

If we collect
the dust from wings
and from our masters
severed strings
and a cup half full
of summer's waning insolence
mix it 'round with our laments
to paint the yellow evening's sky
the colour of our brief regrets
saving from the Sunday feast
our morsel grim and frugal ironies
playing hymns as indistinct
on my crack and crooked radio
as these rainy day blurred windows
I will make a shallow breath
to draw a game of tic tac toe
wondering as I make an x
who upon the other side makes zeros?

Solemn Grace

Solemn Grace breaks Monday morning dishes
in a symphony of final straws and camel backs
Scraped plates make a feast (she says)
for monsters at the corner of the drive
where the cement in jigsaw pieces
crookèd with the pulverising weight
of hard as spite hydraulic tongues
from this once smoothed surface, breach
the ceremonious drumming basso voice
of tossed upended bins
not quite divine
nevertheless, a calendar of sorts
perhaps not so majestic
as solstice dolmen shadows
but still, in the aftermathing silence
in two halves
I am lambent before my father's eyes

Whale Bone Lamp

Annabelle Obscura wears a widow's bun
knotted 'round a hook of whalebone
that her young Captain had
carved with the marks of saints
in a peculiar kind of Braille
that felt like lost promises
of a forgotten summer land

Her fingers leave red marks
like the phases of the moon
when she holds too tight
harpoons crossed around her eyes, saying

Long days are strangely round
chrysanthemums are for the dead
I live somewhere in the houses of your face
– that is a gull-like memory
of course, I feel sorry for the beast
its singing heart pierced through
but how deep it sang!
to offer bones so few
to light a light
while I wait
turning empty cards
in a fading window

Car Crash No.4

I think, the grooves in your face
are deep enough for lost civilisations

We are evening's children
waiting for an amaranth sea to end

You come out of the haze
bent until your ribs have stitched your side

As if a whale bared and writhed
on a sudden shore

Flights tearing in their susurrations
totems, crosses, hubcaps, wreaths

The stitches tattoo black
wreak a journey from a smile

Fallen in and bright
as a roadside memorial

Not knowing why
the arcing traffic
anvil struck and in fast careen

so blindly ignores

We Leave At Ten

We leave at ten
for the northern line
the muring still as hunted birds
quiet as statues (the inept kind)
that scowl and scowl and scowl
but never make a noise

The glass has shaded imagos
of others and the self
peering in as we peer out
jostled lines of luggage
on parallel lines of shelf
with the Damocles threat
of unruly boarders
(we cringe and utter blandishments)
arching statuesque complaints

The day – train long
crosses roads
with crucifixion bells
jangling off and on, the widows
in their voodoo coiffures, scowling
playing mahjong (worn as scrimshaw
in the berth the next along)
the way crows peck at desultory bones
thin as sunset, in their smiles, at the roar
of elements and intersections

We're almost there, she turning says
face hunched, the butterfly, recklessly pinned
to the breakers of her hair
in the half-light, flickering
another shadow passes
pointing, she scrapes a clumsy wing
(we lurch on again)
spilling tiles like the end of sudden rain

Birnam & Amber

I think I remember best of all
how the linoleum hospice cold
in the quiet aftermath
of violent emesis
played a surreptitious game
the black squares swallowing whole
the birnam hush of you footsteps
The white, blinding sharp
in those strange foreshortened parallelograms
as if the Opera House
bit into my face
with that profound crescendo
of spinnakers torn and breaking
in a sideways sea

Stone is for the dead, I say
sinking in the eye
poised above
you have the scent
of fresh-sawn lumber
your hands with that green limb strength

Wood is for the living (you reply)
resin-warm and pouring
a new day through the long forgotten amber
of my insect moment

Reaching, almost gone
you still lift me
like a wandered tree

Neither Read, Nor Yet, Written

Winter's leaving, in piecemeal increments
the sky has the tilt, of neglected volumes
that you thought you'd read one day
Blake, and Howl and that exegesis
on the sailboat shapes of sundials
teetering in monuments, cocooning time

On the verandah, in the darkening afternoon
blue-grey ink in chatter falling
to leave pages raw as skeins

In Japan (I say) they have a word for unread books
I don't remember exactly what it is
the intentionality as beautiful as
a cicada's dream of spring
shoots bare as nibs from naked branches
and petals
soft and veined and blind and
so many days, thick as loaves, drunk as hope
not yet read
not yet written

Train Station Number Nine

My love is a pale horse (she says)
Now far from home, a wretch
and desert heaving
I will gather you to my arms
as bright as childhood fever
swole with milk-white sleep
and the notorious benadryl hum
of cicadas dreaming

The downpour has an intermittent drone
of distended announcements
as if unintelligible trains
were arriving and departing
through an earth made porous

By her predestinations

I will wait   and count
the hubbub a kind of music

Distant and distinct
of life collapsing
til another engine slides
in sonorous ignominy

Here On Midsummer's River, We So Elegantly Fall

At your party I will stand
compliant as a hat rack
carefully holding parasols and scarves
(An iron kind of evening – neither cool nor bright)

You will swan about the room
breaking arms
smiling with an executioner's grace
bodice laced
with an hourglass desperation

I am still angular as adolescence
by the kitchen door
holding these detestable canapés
(pierced through and with an iridescent shine
like the mortised remains
of blue admiral butterflies)

Crying for your midnight emancipation
(your powdered mien begins to crack like glass)
in the bevelled edge of gilded mirrors
catching signs of extraordinary life
for an exit, feint
collapsing in three miles of sequinned cloth

As if you were the last enchanted ave
on midsummer's river

Of course
it is not yet daylight savings here
my hands too full of walking sticks and woollen mittens
I wear my face at 3 a.m. (or quarter past) and watch

Letting you fall slowly to the floor

Harvest

You have lost
your white gloves

Walk with me
through fields of amaranth and wild wheat
they have women's names and men's curses

Take an arrowed stem to your lips
do you taste a world
that counted iron sacred
or just the summer sun
warm as blood beneath the skin
in isthmus dark   as long as history?

How we hide
from summer rain
arms arched above our heads as if
a scythe of love were some protection

You must be a tree
how I rest and hide in you
while birdsong ladders a half-broken sky

I thought I saw your gloves take flight
afraid of my green jealousy
here is gold, here peony
is that what Ophelia said?

From thistle, down, from nettle, balm
rue for memory, pressed to calm
on your lips

your small serpent sting
how in this caduceus   we entwine
for daisy chains, a foolish day of love

Aberdeen Street

On Aberdeen Street
    the steps go up
        and back in time
                    steep work
                        for a man
        with a knot wood cane
        snail-bent and watching
the calligraphy of foot-worn stone

            In the morning dark
a cat shape disappears
                    a sawtooth fear
                        leaves wittering
        a whine in the ear
                a shadow sinters
as quickly gone

Cattle-eyed
            toothed muttering
    a shawl of beetled wings
            stretched against the burgeoning resistance
    of day's upward climb
            they take a stymied flight

  You sour apples
                he says to her
    all crowcraw bright
                forgetting she is gone and bittersweet
        as burnt sugar and cinnamon

She swallows proffered morsels
                head tossed back
        then bird-replies

replete

                        You know a crow is just a songbird
                if you listen past the laughter

with a broken heart

Looking For Yuri Gagarin

Broken bottles on the ground
at every alley mouth
I ask for Yuri Gagarin

Space is what is left
when we are hollowed out
by need sharp as stars

This is just his misnomer
I reply, to the swish of butterfly knives
you will know him by

The darkness in his visor
the shirt he wears blood red
marked in giant leaps

Like slowly turning weapons
the orbit all too brief
the ricochet

A spray of glass
as if these spring-tide petals
bludgeoning your squinted face
were cast in the wind

The grit and garbage soughing
of another voiceless cry
the fishbowl beneath his arm

That I think we live inside
all but empty

You know I have, he says
pockets full of sand
leaking out like time
through the holes and veils

Leaving shore thin strands
so if you chase the wind
you can find me

One For Sorrow

To mourn a magpie broken on the road
Gather her in your clumsy pickpocket hands
Smoothing jigsaw wings
Too awkward to steal away the stillness in her eye
Lay her where the pines will sow a song
In softly falling needles
Where eucalypts in piebald mourning bend
Where her tidings chorus round in wildered silence
On crook and sorrowed branches til they sing
Raise your head and with them sing along
Tooroo tooray karoo kallay kar kalloo kalloo kallay
Tooroo toorah karoo kallay koora kalloo kallay
One for sorrow
Two for wings
Three for laughter
Four for love
Five for summer's soaring days
Six for winter's morning songs

About the Author

C S Hughes grew up by the bellow and stink of cattle yards, and the hollow and roar of dunes. He says he was a hobo in his youth, and later worked as a spice seller, a book dealer, and a trader in junk and assorted detritus.

More recently he has been a writer and editor of poetry books, editing *From The Ashes - Poetry In Support Of Bushfire Relief, The Poetry Of John Ashdown-Hill* and *Somnia Blue,* amongst others.

He has been published online and in print in *Blue Pepper, Five 2 One, Weird Tales, Sampietrino, The Blue Nib* and various others. He has published several collections of his own work, including, *The Little Book Of Funerals, The Book Of Whimsies, The Book Of Barbarous Tales,* the short story collection *The Book Of Fables,* and the novella in verse, *COVID-22.*

He currently lives in the Gippsland Lakes region of Victoria with a cat and an historian, where he (still) studies and dabbles in story writing, but claims, with a nearly straight face, to still mostly being a hobo.

9 780645 920499